This book belongs to

Kiara

....

....

Nita Mehta
PUBLICATIONS

Tell me About
THE SIKHS

© Copyright 2005 *Nita Mehta* PUBLICATIONS

WORLD RIGHTS RESERVED: The contents—all text and illustrations are original and copyrighted. No portion of this book shall be reproduced, stored in a retrieval system or transmitted by any means, electronic, mechanical, photocopying, recording or otherwise, without the written permission of the publishers.

While every precaution is taken in the preparation of this book, the publisher and the author assume no responsibility for errors or omissions. Neither is any liability assumed for damages resulting from the use of information contained herein.

TRADEMARKS ACKNOWLEDGED: Trademarks used, if any, are acknowledged as trademarks of their respective owners. These are used as reference only and no trademark infringement is intended upon.

First Edition 2005
ISBN 81-7676-039-0

Illustrations: *Nita Mehta* PUBLICATIONS

Layout and laser typesetting:

National Information Technology Academy
3A/3, Asaf Ali Road
New Delhi-110002
☎ 23252948

Published by:

Nita Mehta PUBLICATIONS

3A/3 Asaf Ali Road, New Delhi-110002
Tel: 91-11-23250091, 29214011, 23252948, 29218727
Fax: 91-11-29225218, 91-11-23250091
E-Mail : nitamehta@email.com, snab@snabindia.com
Website : http://www.nitamehta.com, http://www.snabindia.com

Distributed by :

THE VARIETY BOOK DEPOT
A.V.G. Bhavan, M 3 Con Circus,
New Delhi - 110 001
Tel : 23417175, 23412567; Fax : 23415335
Email: varietybookdepot@rediffmail.com

Printed by :

AJANTA OFFSET & PACKAGING LTD

Tell Me About
THE SIKHS

ANURAG MEHTA

VANEETA VAID

Nita Mehta
PUBLICATIONS

THE SIKHS

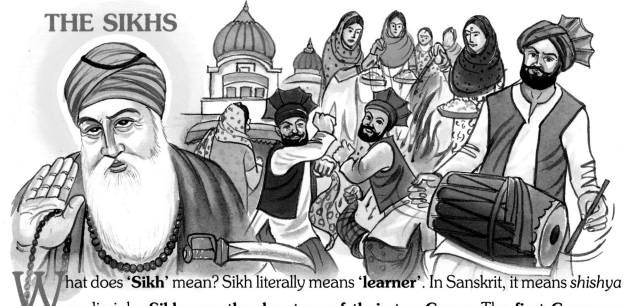

What does **'Sikh'** mean? Sikh literally means **'learner'**. In Sanskrit, it means *shishya* or disciple. **Sikhs are the devotees of their ten Gurus**. The **first Guru** was **Guru Nanak Dev** (1469-1539). He was the founder of the Sikh religion, **Sikhism**. The **tenth and the last Guru** was **Guru Gobind Singh** (1666-1708). The bulk of Sikh people live in the northern state of Punjab although they are spread throughout the world.

GURU NANAK

The Founder of the Sikh Faith

Guru Nanak Dev was born in **1469** in Talwandi, a village in the Sheikhpura district, 65 kilometers west of Lahore (in Pakistan). His father was a village official in the local revenue administration. Even as a child, Guru Nanak was different from other children. He carried around him a divine aura. At school, he learnt things so fast that the teacher thought that he was a genius and would grow up to be a great man. He grew up and got married, but still spent most of his time thinking about God and saying prayers.

Guru Nanak as a child

Nanak leaves home

God's Message to Guru Nanak...

Guru Nanak began to work as a store-keeper and did his job well. His employer was delighted with him but Nanak himself was not happy. Then one night, he had a dream and saw God himself standing before him. "Forgive me, O Lord!" said Nanak. "I have done a great wrong."

"What wrong have you done?" asked the Lord. "I've thought only of this world," he said. "I have worked for money."

"My blessings are with you," said the Lord. "Go out into the world and help all men."

The very next day, Nanak gave up his job. He gave away all his money and possessions. He kept just one piece of clothing to cover himself. He took a bowl so that he could beg for his food, a strong stick to help him in his journey and a mat on which he could sit and say his prayers. He wandered from place to place. He visited many holy places and met many holy men. He wanted to share his views with one and all.

Guru Nanak's Preachings…

"God is one and belongs to us all", said Nanak. "You will not only find him in mosques and temples but also in your heart." He said that a man of religion should do three things.

1. He should earn his living with honest labour and should not lead an idle life.

2. He should share his earnings with others and help the weak.

3. He should always remember God and should ask others to do likewise.

Guru Nanak
Teaching
People

Guru Nanak also believed that a person should lead a normal life. What does that mean? That means that in-spite of devoting our soul to the prayer of the almighty, a person should earn a living, start a family and subsist in a daily every day existence. Whatever is earned, part of that income should be devoted to the 'seva' or welfare of others! Guru Nanak himself was married and was blessed with two sons. He continued tilling his lands as a farmer simultaneously with his spiritual mission. Guru Nanak sang out his preachings like devotional songs. His songs were called **Gurubani** or *the songs of the Guru*.

Guru Nanak Spreads His Faith...

Guru Nanak travelled from village to village conveying his message to people. Many people listened to him and became his followers. His followers came to be known as **Sikhs** and their religion, **Sikhism**.

Some People are Suspicious...

Guru Nanak did not like many customs and practices among both Hindus and Muslims. In his teachings, Guru Nanak reversed the ongoing religious practices and taught a completely new concept of faith. He spoke against the caste system and meaningless practices prevalent in the society in those times. To make his point of the one-ness of society, Guru Nanak wore a combination of the Hindu and Muslim dress! This made the community suspicious and unsettled. Soon a rumble of protest began to gather.

"Go away! How dare you mock our rituals!" was a common protest! But soon, some of the public began to understand his message and his following increased.

An Interesting Tale...

One morning, while Nanak was bathing in the *Ganga* (Ganges), he found people offering handfuls of water to the sun, for honouring the spirits of their departed ancestors.

He went up to a *brahmin* (priest) and asked, "Would this water that you are offering, reach your departed ancestors."

The *brahmin* proudly answered, "Yes, it would."

Hearing this, Guru Nanak began throwing water in the opposite direction. The priests standing nearby objected to this. Nanak replied, "I am sending water to my fields in Punjab, which are nearer than the abode of your ancestors."

The people realised what the Guru was saying. They requested him to show them the right path.

Guru Nanak with the brahmins

Malik Bhago and Lalo...

Another tale that reveals the lesson behind Guru Nanak's teachings is one about Malik Bhago, a rich man and Lalo, a poor farmer. Both of them invited Guru Nanak to stay in their house. The Guru chose to stay in the poor farmer's house and the rich man demanded an explanation for this. Guru Nanak asked him to get some *chappatis* (food) from his house. He also asked Lalo, the poor farmer, to get some food. Then, taking Lalo's *chappatis* in his right hand and Malik Bhago's in his left, he squeezed the two. Everybody present was shocked to see drops of blood coming out of Malik Bhago's *chappatis* and drops of milk from Lalo's *chappatis*. Guru Nanak then told a completely ashamed Malik Bhago that his food was made from the earnings got by torturing and exploiting the poor and the weak, while Lalo's food was made from hard earned money. He advised Malik Bhago to earn by hard work and to serve the needy with a true heart. The guilty man fell at the Guru's feet and begged forgiveness.

Malik bhago and Lalo with
Guru Nanak

Guru Nanak Chooses His Successor...

One of Guru Nanak's wealthy followers gave him some land on the banks of the river Ravi. There the village of **Kartarpur** was built. The Guru lived here till his death in 1539. But, before he died, he chose one of his favourite disciples to carry on his work and thus the tradition of Sikh Gurus began.

Guru Nanak chooses Guru Angad as his successor

THE GURUS AFTER GURU NANAK

Guru Angad Writes the Present form of Gurmukhi...

Guru Angad Dev (1504-1552) became the next spiritual head of the Sikhs after Guru Nanak. He is credited with the present form of the **Gurmukhi** script. What is Gurmukhi? It is and was the medium of writing the Punjabi language in which the hymns of the Gurus were expressed. These scriptures were made available to the common people so they began to call it *Gurumukhi*.

Guru Angad

Be Active...

Like Guru Nanak, Guru Angad also believed every one in the community should be energized and active. There was no place for laziness and idleness!

Guru Amardas Continues the Sikh Faith...

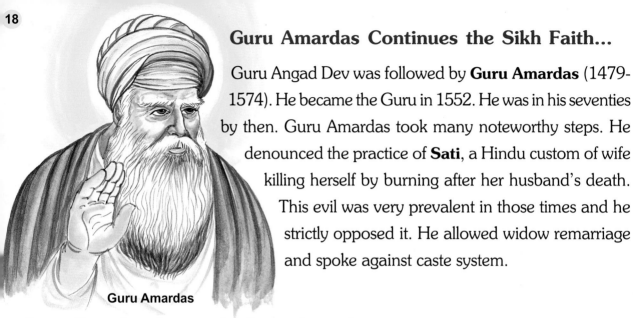

Guru Angad Dev was followed by **Guru Amardas** (1479-1574). He became the Guru in 1552. He was in his seventies by then. Guru Amardas took many noteworthy steps. He denounced the practice of **Sati**, a Hindu custom of wife killing herself by burning after her husband's death. This evil was very prevalent in those times and he strictly opposed it. He allowed widow remarriage and spoke against caste system.

Guru Amardas

Guru Ramdas Succeeds Guru Amardas...

Guru Amardas passed on his Guru ship to his son in law, Ramdas Sodhi, who was his most devoted disciple. **Guru Ramdas** became the **fourth** Sikh Guru.

Guru Ramdas

The Lake of Nectar and the City of Amritsar...

Guru Ramdas began to set up a temple near Lahore, which could be looked upon by the followers as the seat of spiritual and temporal authority of the Guru. This temple was called the Harimandir and later the Harmindar Saab. A pool of water was dug around the Harmindar Saab so that devotees could purify themselves before offering prayers in the temple. This lake was called the Amrit-Sarovar (lake of nectar). The city which developed around it was named 'Amritsar'.

Although Guru Ramdas started building the Harmindar Saab, it was completed by **Guru Arjan Dev.** Arjan Dev was his son who also became the **fifth** Sikh Guru.

Guru Arjan Dev gives Sikhs a Separate Identity...

Guru Arjan Dev slowly gave Sikhism a separate identity from Hinduism and Islam. Guru Arjan Dev was the youngest son of Guru Ramdas. He was born at Goindwal and became Guru at the young age of 18 in 1581. He married and had one son. He also completed the building of the Hari Mandir or Harmindar Saab, now known as the **Golden Temple**, in the middle of the pool or the lake of nectar.

The Adi Granth is Compiled...

Guru Arjan remained the Guru for fifteen years. He is also credited with the actual compilation of the Adi Granth, later to be called **Guru Granth Sahib**. He collected the hymns of the previous Gurus into one large volume. His predecessor, Guru Amardas had already worked on preliminary collection of the hymns by the earlier Gurus. Guru Arjan gave it a concrete shape dividing the hymns according to their author and the type of composition and music. After the Gurus, the Adi Granth became very important as it represented the Gurus.

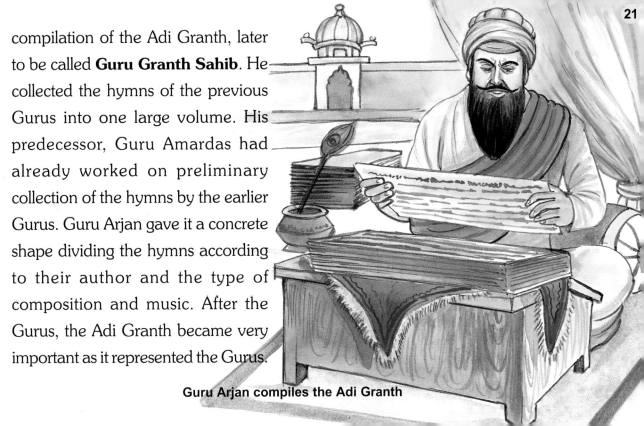

Guru Arjan compiles the Adi Granth

The Ruling Mughals get Insecure...

What was the political situation then? The Mughal Emperor **Jehangir** was reigning. He was very disturbed by the rapid spread of Sikhism. Guru Arjan Dev was accused and arrested for helping one of the rebellious princes. He was tortured so badly that Guru Arjan Dev died in the Mughal prison. Guru Arjan Dev became the first of a long list of Sikh martyrs.

Guru Hargobind Changes the Face of Sikhism...

Guru Hargobind succeeded Guru Arjan Dev as the **Sixth** Guru. Guru Hargobind transformed the direction of the community by organizing them into an army! From being a purely religious group, the Sikhs transformed themselves into an armed group capable of defending themselves. On his anointment as the Guru, Hargobind declared, "I will wear two swords! One for spiritual power and one for temporal. I shall combine the two to face tyranny!"

Guru Hargobind with followers

What tyranny? The tyranny of the Mughals of course. These rulers were forcing everyone to convert to Islam. Since the Sikhs were resisting, they were being butchered mercilessly. The guru also decided to have a kingdom, strong enough to stand against outside forces.

The Building of the Akal Takht...

Guru Hargobind built the Akal Takht. This is a building opposite the Harmindar Sahib, which houses the Takht. 'Takht' means a throne or seat. Akal Takht is the seat of the highest-ranking decision-maker of the Sikhs. There are five Akal Takhts all over India but the one at the Golden Temple in Amritsar is the most important. Today they are considered the center of Sikh religious authority and are binding for Sikhs worldwide.

The Mughals Make Life for the Sikhs Difficult...

Times were bad for the Sikhs under the leadership of Guru Hargobind. They had to face the oppression of the Mughal forces. Four major battles ensued. The Sikhs fought with such raw courage and determination that even though they were greatly outnumbered, they defeated the Mughal forces in every battle. According to the Mughal rulers, the militancy of the Sikhs was harmful to the security of the Mughal Empire. This resulted in the ferocious repression of the Sikhs by the Mughals.

Guru Har Rai and Dara Shikoh...

The **seventh** guru of the Sikh faith was Guru Har Rai (1630-1661). When Guru Har Rai grew up, he kept an army but never fought a battle. Apart from rejuvenating the Sikh faith, this Guru impressed Dara Shikoh. Who was Dara Shikoh? He was the brother of the ruling Mughal Emperor Aurangzeb. Aurangzeb and Dara could not see eye to eye and because of this Dara fled. Dara entered the Punjab and he called on Guru Har Rai. Prince Dara was of a freethinking temperament and had a natural inclination for the company of pious persons. Unfortunately, Dara's meeting with Guru Har Rai was distorted to the Emperor Aurangzeb. He was given the impression that Guru Har Rai was deliberately teasing him by aligning with his estranged brother! In anger, he called Guru Har Rai to his court. Guru Har Rai refused to be intimidated by this call. However, not ignoring the call completely, Guru Har Rai sent his son Ram Rai instead!

Dara Shikoh

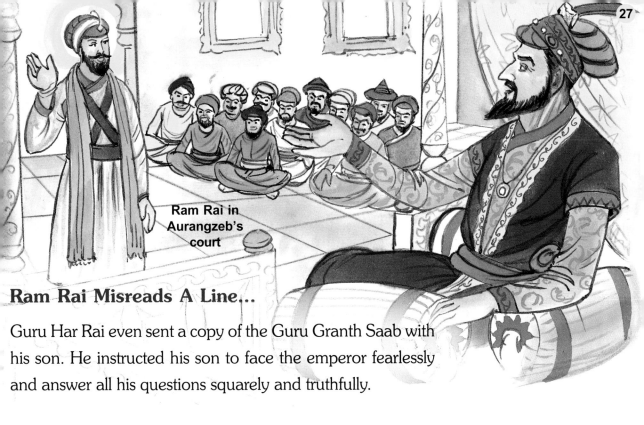

Ram Rai in Aurangzeb's court

Ram Rai Misreads A Line...

Guru Har Rai even sent a copy of the Guru Granth Saab with his son. He instructed his son to face the emperor fearlessly and answer all his questions squarely and truthfully.

However, Ram Rai deliberately misread one of the lines from the (Guru) Granth Sahib. Now why would he do that? Well, it is said that Ram Rai was trying to please the emperor! On his return, Ram Rai, was expelled from presence of Guru Har Rai for this misconduct. Guru Har Rai chose his younger son, Har Krishan, to be his successor and had him anointed as Guru.

Guru Har Krishan

Guru Har Krishan...

Guru Har Rai passed away on October 6, 1661. Guru Har Krishan who succeeded him, was also called the 'child guru' as he became the guru at the age of five. This guru was also troubled by the Mughal emperor Aurangzeb. Aurangzeb insisted that the Sikh Guru perform miracles and feats in his court. "If you are a mystique, show me miracles!" declared Auranzeb.

Guru Har Krishan refused. He believed that no one should attempt a mirage and try to disturb the law of God. Guru Har Krishan displayed great spiritual leadership and courage even at such a young age! Unfortunately, Guru Har Krishan died very early. Before his death at the age of eight, he nominated **Guru Tegh Bahadur** as his successor.

Guru Tegh Bahadur Helps the Hindus...

Auranzeb asked Guru Teg Bhadur to embrace Islam if he could not show miracles! On the other hand, Hindu Brahmins pleaded with Guru Tegh Bahadur to help them from the attack by the Muslim rulers, who were forcibly converting all Hindus to Islam.

Guru Tegh Bahadur journeyed to Delhi to reason with the Emperor.

Guru Tegh Bahadur

At Emperor Aurangzeb's Court...

At Delhi, Guru Tegh Bahadur was brought to an open place of execution. The emperor ordered Guru Tegh Bahadur to accept Islam or death. Guru Tegh Bahadur gave him a fitting answer. He said, "Hinduism may not be my faith and I may not believe in their sacred thread, caste system and idol worship, but I will fight for the right of all Hindus to live with honour and freedom to practice their faith according to their beliefs." Enraged Auranzeb tortured the Guru and then killed him. Once again a martyr was born, who gave up his life to preserve the sanctity of his faith.

Guru Gobind Singh Fights Tryanny...

Gobind Rai succeeded Guru Tegh Bahadur at the tender age of nine. He was Guru Tegh Bahadur's son. Guru Gobind made Sikhism into an active movement to fight the dictatorship and injustice of emperor Aurangzeb.

Guru Gobind Singh

His goal was to create a nation that would be pure and strong enough to free itself from the oppression of priests and rulers alike! Guru Gobind thought how he should shape his Sikhs into such a force that none could withstand it.

The Creation of the Khalsa...

On the day of Baisakhi, 13th April 1699, a significant incident took place. Guru Gobind assembled his Sikhs numbering 200,000 - 250,000, at Anandpur (at the foothills of the Sivaliks). He asked for five volunteers from the throng. They came forth. Guru Gobind baptized the five disciples from different castes with Amrit or nectar. The Five Beloved became the first members of the brotherhood of the *Khalsa*, or the pure. The word *Khalsa* comes from the Sanskrit word *khaals,* meaning pure. Those five Sikhs were the first to be instructed about the *Khalsa* community. Guru Gobind Singh called them *"Panj Pyare"*, the five devoted spirits beloved of the Guru.

Creation of the Khalsa

Surnames for the Sikhs...

The last names of the five were replaced by the suffix 'Singh' meaning lion. This was to apply for all the Sikhs there on. The ladies names were suffixed by 'Kaur', meaning princess Lioness. By this move, all caste barriers were removed! Thus, Gobind Rai became SRI GURU GOBIND SINGH.

The Five 'K's...

Guru Gobind Singh declared the five emblems of the Sikhs at this meeting. They were the five 'K's. These were: **Kesh** (uncut hair), **Kangha** (comb), **Kara** (a metal wristband), **Kirpan** (sword) and **Kachha** (undergarment shorts) . These five symbols were to become the identity of being a true 'Khalsa' Sikh.

Kesh

Kirpan

Kangha

Kachha

Kara

Fight with the Mughals Continues...

Guru Gobind Singh was like a storm for the Mughal oppressors. He moved from place to place fighting the Mughals. Most of his life was spent on horseback. It would be proper to say that it was he who kindled the spirit of independence among Indians in Punjab to fight Muslim tyranny! Guru Gobind Singh transformed the Sikhs from being just spiritual and pious followers of the Guru into fierce fighters against Mughal subjugation.

After Guru Gobind Singh ascended to the heavens in 1708, his ardent follower, Banda Singh Bahadur (1670-1716) a Hindu ascetic converted to Sikhism set about trying to create a Sikh homeland in Punjab.

The Guru Granth Sahib is the Eleventh Guru...

Guru Granth Sahib was appointed as the Eleventh Guru by the Tenth Guru, Guru Gobind Singh. He had instructed his disciples that there would be no guru after him. The Guru Granth Sahib was to be referred to for all religious and spiritual matters.

So after he passed away, the Guru Granth Sahib, which is the holy book of the Sikhs, was given the position of a living Guru. It is the ultimate teacher of the Sikhs.

Guru Granth has 1430 pages of text in poetry form. The Guru Granth is full of devotion, meditation, grace of the Guru and God. It includes hymns of more than 20 Hindu and Muslim saints of India. It is the only holy book in the world, which was written by its founder of religion. Guru Granth Sahib is a Granth (book) originally compiled by the Fifth Guru and named as Adi Granth and later recompiled by all the gurus that followed him.

Banda Singh Bahadur...

The first bid for establishing the Khalsa Raj was made by Banda Singh Bahadur, Guru Gobind Singh's ardent follower! He was not very successful though. Banda was a resolute and strong leader but the Mughal Army proved too many and Banda could not succeed in freeing the country from their oppressive rule. He and his 740 followers were tortured to death.

Maharaja Ranjit Singh...

Later, a daring young boy called Ranjit Singh united the Sikhs and turned them into great people. He was short, frail and had only one eye. Yet he was a born fighter and an excellent horseman. At the age of 18, he became the ruler of Lahore. Soon, he added Amritsar, Multan, Peshawar and some places beyond it to his kingdom.

Maharaja Ranjit Singh

The Golden Temple...

Maharaja Ranjit repaired the Harmindar Sahib that had been burnt down by the Afghan invader Ahmed Shah Abdali. He rebuilt the temple in marble and covered its domes with gold. This is how it came to be known as THE GOLDEN TEMPLE.

The Treaty of Amritsar…

By this time, the British were the masters of the whole of India except the Punjab. Ranjit Singh was a wise man and recognized the growing power of the British. To maintain the sovereignty of his kingdom, he signed the treaty of Amritsar with the British on April 25, 1809. After the treaty with British, Maharaja Ranjit Singh was made master of almost the entire territory to the west of Sutluj. Ranjit Singh ruled for 40 years and worked hard to make the Sikhs a mighty power.

The Sikh kingdom survived for some years after the passing away of Ranjit Singh. After his death in 1839, the British defeated the Sikh forces at Chillianwalla and annexed the kingdom.

Golden Temple

SIKHS IN THE MODERN WORLD

During the freedom struggle of India, the Sikhs showed raw courage in the face of British oppression. Many Sikhs bore brutalities, bullets and long term imprisonments in order to liberate India. The Sikhs constitute only 2.2 percent of India's population. However, there are Sikhs in almost every country in the world and the population of Sikhs is growing. In the United Kingdom, there are almost two hundred Gurudwaras! In fact, in some countries, the Sikh community even has political representation in governments! This hard working community has made a distinctive place for itself wherever it has gone. Today there are around 20 million Sikhs in the world!

THE TRADITIONS AND SYMBOLS OF THE SIKHS

Langar…

The institution of *langar* was started by Guru Nanak. Its need was felt to provide food for visitors and devotees who came to meet Guru Nanak.

The kitchen came to be known as *Guru-ka-langar*. The ingredients needed to cook the meals came from the lands, which Guru Nanak had tilled with the help of his devotees! During the time of Guru Amardas, the third Guru, this system created a sense of equality and brotherhood amongst all. Every one regardless of caste or creed sat in a line and partook food together. No one could meet the Guru without first taking his meal in the *langar*.

The Gurdwara...

The Sikh place of worship is called *Gurudwara*. Historically, it has also served as a refuge for the homeless, the helpless and the destitute, no matter what their religion; with the only requirement that they remove their shoes and cover their head.

Seva...

Seva is very important to the Sikh faith. Seva means voluntary service for the upkeep of the Gurudwara. It includes sweeping and plastering the floors of the Gurdwara, serving water to or fanning the congregation, dusting the shoes of the people visiting the Gurdwara, offering provisions to and rendering any kind of service in the common kitchen-cum-eating house.

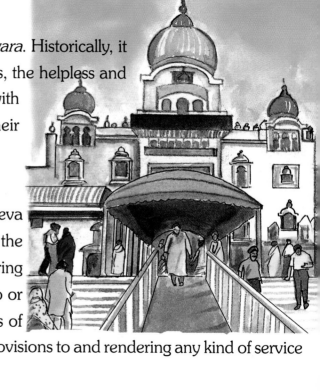

Nishan Saab...

Gurdwaras usually display and fly the Nishan Sahib, a yellow (saffron) triangular flag bearing the Sikh symbol of Khanda (Sword) in blue colour in the center.

Wahe Guru Ji Ka Khalsa, Wahe Guru Ji Ki Fateh...

This salutation was introduced by command of guru Gobind Singh in 1699 when the khalsa was created. What does it mean? This Sikh salutation means "Khalsa belongs to God and to God alone belongs the victory".

Sat Sri Akal...

Is a form of Sikh greeting. It means: "This remembers one and others to live with truth, achieve all treasures and merge in eternity".

Guru Nanak Jayanti or Gurupurab...

The Sikhs celebrate ten Gurupurabs in a year. Each Gurupurab marks either the birth, death or martyrdom days of the Sikh Gurus. The most significant Gurpurab is that of the birth anniversary of Gurunanak.

Baisakhi or Vaisaki...

On this day, the Tenth Guru, Guru Gobind Singh created the Khalsa. Baisakhi is celebrated on 13th April every year. On this day, the Sikhs come together in the Gurdwara to offer prayers. They also take part in serving the free meal or 'Langar'. The typical 'Halwa' is distributed as 'Prasad'. Yellow colour clothes are also worn to denote the colours of the harvesting month.